Withdrawn

D1072627

Under the Sea
1,2,3
An Ocean Counting Book

by Tracey E. Dils

AMICUS READERS 1 AMICUS INK

Say Hello to Amicus Readers.

You'll find our helpful dog, Amicus, chasing a ball—to let you know the reading level of a book.

1
Learn to Read
Frequent repetition, high frequency words, and close photo-text matches introduce familiar topics and provide ample support for brand new readers.

2
Read Independently
Some repetition is mixed with varied sentence structures and a select amount of new vocabulary words are introduced with text and photo support.

3
Read to Know More
Interesting facts and engaging art and photos give fluent readers fun books both for reading practice and to learn about new topics.

Amicus Readers and Amicus Ink are imprints of Amicus
P.O. Box 1329, Mankato, MN 56002
www.amicuspublishing.us

Library of Congress Cataloging-in-Publication Data
Dils, Tracey E., author.
  Under the sea 1, 2, 3 : an ocean counting book / by Tracey E. Dils.
    1 online resource. -- (1, 2, 3... count with me)
  Summary: "Introduces whales, sharks, sea stars, and other animals of the sea, while teaching the concept of counting to ten"-- Provided by publisher.
  Audience: Grades K to 3.
  Description based on print version record and CIP data provided by publisher; resource not viewed.
  ISBN 978-1-60753-717-5 (library binding)
  ISBN 978-1-60753-821-9 (ebook)
  ISBN 978-1-68152-005-6 (paperback)
  1. Counting--Juvenile literature. 2. Marine animals--Juvenile literature. I. Title.
  QA113
  513.2'11--dc23
                    2014046824

Photo Credits: Rich Carey/Shutterstock Images, cover (background), 14-15, 16-17 (foreground); Shutterstock Images, cover (left top), cover (right), 1, 3, 12 (bottom), 12 (top right), 13 (bottom), 14 (left), 15 (top left), 24 (top right, bottom left), 24 (top right, top right); Serg Dibrova/Shutterstock Images, cover (left bottom); Konrad Mostert/Shutterstock Images, 4; Quinn Martin/Shutterstock Images, 6-7, 24 (bottom right); Ethan Daniels/Shutterstock Images, 9; Rostislav Ageev/Shutterstock Images, 8; Willyam Bradberry/Shutterstock Images, 10-11, 24 (top left); iStock/Thinkstock, 12-13; Maryna Kulchytska/Shutterstock Images, 12 (top left); Elena Schweitzer/Shutterstock Images, 13 (top); Nantawat Chotsuwan/Shutterstock Images, 14 (right), 15 (bottom), 24 (top right, middle); Adam Lazar/iStockphoto, 14 (middle), 15 (top right), 24 (top left), 24 (bottom right); iStockphoto, 16-17 (background), 18-19 (foreground); Dudarev Mikhail/Shutterstock Images, 18-19 (background); Edwin Verin/Shutterstock Images, 20-21, 24 (bottom left); Levent Konuk/Shutterstock Images, 22-23

Produced for Amicus by The Peterson Publishing Company and Red Line Editorial.

Editor Jenna Gleisner
Designer Craig Hinton

Printed in Malaysia
HC 10 9 8 7 6 5 4 3 2 1
PB 10 9 8 7 6 5 4 3 2 1

All kinds of animals live under the sea. Let's count them!

3

Three lobsters crawl on the ocean floor. They live near coral reefs.

4

Four dolphins swim. They talk to each other with clicks and squeaks.

5

Five sea stars lie on the ocean floor. Each one has five arms.

Six sea horses float. They use a small fin on their backs to swim.

7

Seven sharks look for food. Grey reef sharks eat fish, crabs, and squids.

8

Eight stingrays flap their fins. Their fins give them a flat, round shape.

9

Nine jellyfish float in the water. Jellyfish never stop growing. Some grow as big as a lion!

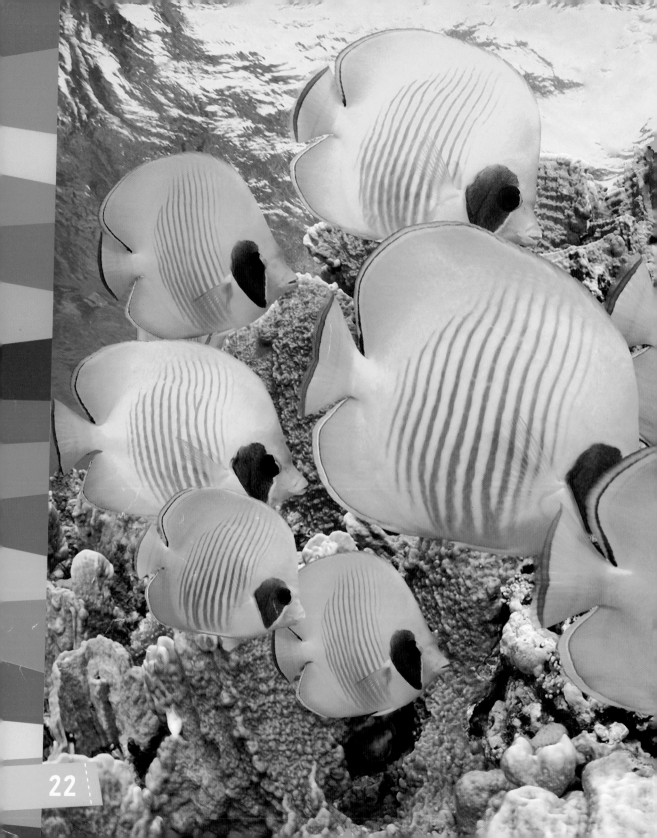

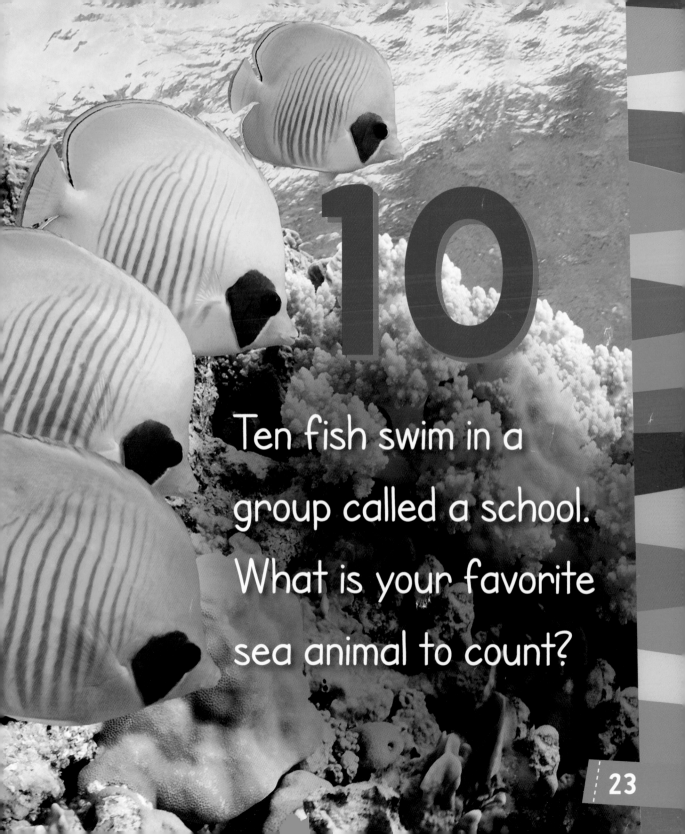

10

Ten fish swim in a group called a school. What is your favorite sea animal to count?

Count Again

Count the number of objects in each box.